A Play

Pamela Boyd

Red Deer College Press

The Publishers
Red Deer College Press
56 Avenue & 32 Street Box 5005
Red Deer Alberta T4N 5H5 Canada

Edited for the Press by Joyce Doolittle
Cover art by Scott Barham
Design by Dennis Johnson
Printed and bound in Canada for Red Deer College Press

Financial support provided by the Alberta Foundation for the Arts, a beneficiary of the Lottery Fund of the Government of Alberta, the Canada Council, the Department of Communication and Red Deer College.

The Alberta Foundation for the Arts

COMMITTED TO THE DEVELOPMENT OF CULTURE AND THE ARTS

CANADIAN CATALOGUING IN PUBLICATION DATA
Boyd, Pamela, 1947–
Odd fish
A play.
ISBN 0-88995-124-1
I. Title.
PS8553.0926032 1994 C812'.54 C94-910304-7
PR9199.3.B69032 1994

LIBRARY OF CONGRESS CATALOGUING IN PUBLICATION DATA
Boyd, Pamela, 1947–
Odd fish / by Pamela Boyd.
p. cm.
ISBN 0-88734-281-7
1. Man-woman relationships—Canada—Drama.
2. Married women—Canada—Drama.
3. Czechs—Canada—Drama.
I. Title.
PR9199.3.B642033 1994
812'.54—dc20

The author acknowledges the assistance of the Ontario Arts Council and the Saskatchewan Writers Guild. With special thanks to Petre Hajek and Ales and Jeronym Brezina.

ODD FISH was originally performed at the Alberta Theatre Projects' playRites '92 Festival, Calgary, Alberta, with the following cast:

Jana	Darcy Dunlop
Ted	Daryl Shuttleworth
Bear	Matthew Woodward
Edwin	Robert Benson
Suza	Kate Newby
Mirek	James Kirchner
Director	Katherine Kaszas
Set and Lighting Design	Warren Carrie and Terry Gunvordahl
Costume Design	Gary Thorne
Sound Design	Allan Rae
Production Dramaturge	Daniel Libman

CHARACTERS

Jana Pavlova	Forties. Emigrated from Czechoslovakia to Canada as a political refuge in 1971.
Ted Miller	Forties. Jana's husband and co-owner of Jana's Landing, a marina.
Bear	Their son, 13 years old.
Suza	Their daughter, 16 years old.
Edwin	A neighbour, midsixties, Anglo-Irish.
Mirek Sling	Forties. An ex-lover of Jana, recently come from Czechoslovakia.

THE ACTION of the play takes place in and around Jana's Landing, the Miller home and adjoining tackle and baitshop on Crystal Lake in the Canadian Shield.

ACT ONE—Thanksgiving Monday, 1990.

ACT TWO—One week later.

OVERLAPPING LINES are indicated by *.

ACT ONE SCENE ONE

Jana's Landing, a fishing retreat in Ontario.

Exterior. Night. Full moon.

Dim light up and continually shifting to reveal a moonlit glade of tall, standing shapes. They are unclear and changeable. They could be trees or totem poles or standing stones or statues. Abstract sound that is reminiscent of cold wind through pine trees.

A real light is switched on upstage. Ted is standing in the doorway of the baitshop, looking into the centre of the glade. Light in the glade continues its shifting, and we see that one of the shapes is Jana, apparently standing in midair, holding something in her cupped hands.

Ted Jan?

No change.

Jan?

She looks up, confused. The light shifts. Ted moves slowly down the dock toward her.

Jan? Come on, Jan.

Jana Dali mi cibuli. Oni se na me divaji. *(They gave me an onion. They are watching me.)*

As Ted moves closer, the light shifts, becoming more real.

Ted Jan. It's Ted. Wake up.

Jana is standing at the very end of the dock, wearing a nightgown and sweater, the lake beneath her. Ted carefully touches her. She star-

tles, and he quickly puts his arms around her, steering her from the edge.

Gees, Jan!

Ted is in rumpled worn sweatpants and half awake. He steers her back up the dock toward the baitshop and sits her on a bench.

Gees!

Ted looks at Jana for a moment, then sits beside her and puts his arm around her.

You're gonna scare the living shit right out of me, you know that?

A cloud covers the moon.

What were you doing at the end of the dock?

Jana The . . . ?

Ted You were standing at the end of the dock.

Silence.

Jana I had a dream.

Ted No kidding.

Pause.

So?

Jana shakes her head.

You awake now? Come on, it's cold as hell.

They go inside through the baitshop to the living room.

Jana stands in the middle of the room. The moon flits in and out from behind clouds.

You okay?

Jana Mmmmmm.

Ted C'mon. Let's go back to bed.

Jana The moon is . . .

She watches the light. The moon disappears.

It was a clearing in the woods . . . was it?

Ted Can we do this in bed?

Jana I was holding something, it was very important.

Jana sits. Ted sighs, sits beside her, puts his arm around her.

Ted Yes?

Jana I was struggling. . . . You know that feeling, it's very important, you must do something, but you can't move. . . . I was holding something, I had to . . . to . . . I was trying to . . .

Ted Yeh? *(yawning)*

Jana It was an onion. They gave me an onion, Ted.

Ted Who?

Jana They did. I don't know. . . . Shadows. No faces.

Ted Yeh?

Jana They gave me an onion, for God's sake, how . . . how absurd. It was all sort of papery, the outer layers. Peeling.

Ted Yeh?

Jana That's all . . . I think.

Ted What was inside?

Jana Inside? I don't know.

Ted Didn't you peel back the layers?

Jana I woke up. You woke me up.

Ted Oh, too bad.

Jana Yes. It should have been your dream. Inside would have been a mathematical equation . . . laughing at you. You would have been angry.

Ted laughs. Jana snuggles up.

Such a tiny little dream, to bring me all the way outside. I wonder what it means.

Ted Right. . . . Mmmmmm, you're warm, how come you're so warm?

Jana An onion, Ted. What does it mean? An onion is so mundane. . . . Or is it?

Ted Got me.

Pause.

Jana Ted?

Ted What?

Jana Nothing.

Ted C'mon Jan, I can't figure out your subconscious.

Jana Well, at least . . .

Ted And dreams are one thing. I can handle dreams. Maybe. But this sleepwalking business scares me to death.

Jana Was I really at the end of the dock?

Ted You were.

Jana Better put a bell around my neck.

Ted Right.

Jana Maybe tie me up.

Ted C'mon you. Let's go to bed. I'm freezing.

Jana But why, why that?

Ted What?

Jana The onion.

Ted How should I know?

Jana I mean, why not . . . ?

Ted What?

Jana An egg.

Ted I thought it was an onion.

Jana I had an egg once, when I was little . . . bright colours, painted . . . flowers, patterns, stars, and inside another, painted also, and another, about six, I think. In the middle was a tiny wooden doll, a peasant girl with rosy cheeks. It was old and worn, and one half of one of the eggs was missing. I used to think where that piece was. It was from the Soviet Union, the egg. I used to imagine that piece lying, secretly, silently somewhere far, far away across the snow, in Siberia.

Ted What's this got to do with . . . ?

Jana Later, when I got older, I lost the little doll in the middle.

Ted What are you talking about, Jan?

Jana Folk art. Why are you so stupid?

Ted Sorry. Why are you so weird?

Jana Okay! All around there were . . . tall shapes, trees . . . but maybe not trees . . . guards maybe or . . . and they kept their faces from me. I know they gave me the onion.

Ted yawns. Jana looks at him and sighs.

Ted What the hell do you want from me?

Jana Just go with me, that's all. Explore. Adventure.

Ted I'm tired and cold, and I don't know what you're talking about.

Jana The mind, the inside, it's a mysterious place to explore. Open up, go with me. We can spectaculate!

Ted Spectaculate?

Jana Of course. You know. When you go for gold or silver or diamonds, for mining. . . . You don't know but . . .

Ted Speculate.

Jana No. Speculate? No. Spectaculate, it's much better, no?

Ted Yeh, spectaculate is definitely better. Gees, Jan, you are so bloody convoluted. How am I . . . I can't . . .

Jana The onion, remember? The onion?

Ted Well, gees, uh, let's see, uh, just give me a sec. . . . You, um, your . . . ancestors are trying to communicate with you. An ancient recipe for turkey stuffing.

Jana laughs.

Jana You are such a mindless jerk, a stupid old scientist. You don't take me seriously, do you?

Ted I do, I do, believe me.

Ted begins kissing Jana's neck.

Jana You might be missing something. You never know, it might be important, it might be the key to . . . to . . .

Ted's kissing is tickling Jana's neck.

Hey . . . hey . . . to the universe . . . to all life . . .

Ted Indubitably. . . . Mmmmmm, yes, mmmmmm . . . the important thing right now is . . . is this . . . universe . . . right here. . . . Mmmmmmm, warmth, body warmth . . . it's invading my brain cells and driving me crazy.

Jana wraps her arms around him. His hand slides up her body to her breast. In a moment he starts to pull away and get up.

Come on.

Jana Mmmmmm. . . .

Jana pulls Ted back down on top of her. She slides her hand down his back and under his sweatpants.

Ted You are such a cheap date.

Jana And you're not?

Ted Bed.

He attempts to get up from the couch.

Jana Mmmmmm, Ted.

They tussle. He gets up and pulls her with him, heading towards the bedroom. The moon comes out from behind a cloud. Jana sees it, hesitates, lets Ted's hand slide out of hers as he exits. She stands looking at the moonlight, walks into it and plays with the shadows. Ted stands in the doorway looking at her.

Ted Jan?

Jana Yes, I'm coming.

He exits, resigned.

Stiny. Stiny bez tvare. *(Shadows. Shadows without faces.)*

Light returns to the surreal glade, and Jana stands in the centre, turning round and round. Wind sounds up. Fade to black.

SCENE TWO

Interior of Miller home. Morning.

Bear enters with the newspaper. He gets himself breakfasst, sets the paper on the table, finds the comics, reads and eats. Jana enters with a large turkey, puts it down and stands looking at it. She is dressed to go out—rubber boots, sweater, etc.

Bear Ma?

Jana kisses him absently then starts to prepare and stuff the turkey. Ted enters with a coffee pot and stands looking at Jana with some surprise.

She's going fishing.

Ted looks at Bear. Bear taps his temple, indicating superior intelligence.

And I'm minding the store, right?

Jana smiles at him.

Silence.

Ted pours himself coffee and takes some of the newspaper from Bear.

Ted You hear Suze come in?

Ted looks at Jana. No response.

Bear Yeh. Ten thirty. Gord brought her. You seen her?

Ted When?

Bear Yesterday.

Ted No. Why?

Bear glances at Jana.

Bear Wait for it.

Ted What are you talking about?

Bear Nothing.

Ted opens the newspaper, holds up Bear's own comic drawings.

Ted Hey, what's this?

Bear Oh! That's mine.

Bear reaches for the drawings.

Ted Wait a minute.

Ted flips through them.

"The Crystal County Chemical Disaster." Hey, this is good, this is real good, Bear. Who's that? . . . Oh, it's Fred.

Ted laughs.

Boy! That's great. . . . Sneaky grin and smell and everything . . . and the county office, and there's Myrtle. . . . Oh, gees, look at Myrtle. That's great, Bear. Better not let her see this. Where's the dump?

Bear shows him.

"Fred Parrot's Secret Dumpsite." Wow! PCBs, chlorine . . . I don't think there was chlorine. . . . What's that? Dio–blob–er–ite?

Bear Yeh, well I can't remember what they all were.

Ted So look 'em up.

Bear Aw, come on, Dad.

Bear grabs a pencil.

Ted Let's see, there was . . . Phenol, with a Ph. There was Vinyl Chloride and Cresols, and, uh, what else? how 'bout Methyl Ethyl Ketone?

Bear I never heard that one before.

Ted Same family and it's a good name, eh. Oh, dear, look at them poor fish, and the raccoon. You seen this, Jan?

Jana is absorbed in stuffing the turkey.

Jan?

Bear She's seen it. K–E–Y–T–O–N–E? That right?

Ted No Y. Yoohoo, Jan!

Jana Straze nebo spehove, odvratily ode me sve tvare. . . . *(Guards or oppressors, they turned their faces from me. . . .)*

Stunned silence.

What was the question?

Ted Nothing, just an article of Bear's in the *Toronto Star* this morning.

Jana Oh.

Bear Dad.

They laugh.

Jana What?

Ted Just kidding.

Jana goes back to stuffing the turkey. Offstage, Suza begins practice on the violin—scales, arpeggios, etc.

So, you still doing your science projects on PCBs?

Bear Yeh. That's it.

Ted This?

He holds up the comics.

Bear Yeh.

Ted Yeh? Your teacher gonna go for that?

Bear It's factual, it's accurate. It's a documentary comic strip.

Ted I guess.

Jana has picked up an onion. She begins to peel off the outer layers with studied interest.

Bear But I might change to tent caterpillars.

Ted pours a cup of coffee for Jana and takes it to her.

Ted Jan?

Jana Mmmm?

Ted It's only a dream.

Jana Mmmm.

Ted Just forget it.

Jana Ted!

Ted Well, it's too . . .

Jana What?

Ted Weird. Don't blow it out of perspective, eh. Keep your feet on the ground.

Jana It's my dream.

Ted Sure.

Jana It could be helpful.

Ted What the hell with?

Suza's practicing gets louder.

Ted Suza! It's eight thirty in the morning, for Pete's sake.

Suza continues playing.

Jana With me. My life. With us. Who knows?

Ted It's an onion, for God's sake.

Jana And it means something. What's the matter, Ted Miller? Spectaculation is too scary for you?

Ted Jan, please. Suza!

Suza makes a loud, rude sound on the violin and stops.

Jana Which is the most scary-scary—that there is something inside or that there is nothing inside the onion?

Ted Now you're being ridiculous.

Jana Oh, Ted, why do you turn to stone every time I try to talk about something other than fishing tackle and boats?

Ted There you go again, you see. You always do this. There's lots of things I let you talk about.

Bear sniggers.

What's the matter with you?

Bear Nothing.

Ted Listen you, I got four boats left to get out of the water this morning. . . .

Bear and Jana burst out laughing.

Well, I do.

They laugh harder.

But later we're gonna do a load of firewood, you and me.

Bear Oh, yea. *(facetious)* What's Suza doing?

Jana Cleaning bait tanks.

Bear She'll love that. Do I gotta do hunting licenses?

Jana Excuse me?

Bear Is it required that I do hunting licenses?

Jana No, it is not required. They are all gone.

Bear Good. Only canoes, huh?

Jana Yah.

Edwin enters through the baitshop, waving a magazine.

Edwin I say, have you seen this, Jan? There's to be an exhibition. Take a look, it's jolly interesting.

Ted Top of the morning to you, Edwin.

Edwin I wish you wouldn't say that, Ted. Irish people never say "top of the morning." . . . Look at this, Jan. It's an exhibition of . . .

Ted Breakfast, Edwin? Coffee?

Edwin What? Oh . . . uh, no . . . yes, coffee please. Now pay attention, Jan. It's from Prague. "A photographic journal recording the communist suppression and destruction of post-invasion artwork done by an underground artist colony striving to stay culturally alive after the 1968 Soviet invasion." . . . And look at that picture. . . .

He hands her the magazine.

That's just about the time you made your escape, isn't it? These'll be your colleagues, won't they? I mean, mightn't some of your own work be . . . ? Well, your work was . . . I mean . . .

Silence.

Devastating picture, eh what?

Jana I know this picture.

Bear Let's see.

Ted and Bear look Jana's shoulder.

That's a Russian soldier, right, Ma?

Jana No, it's not, it's a policeman.

Bear What's he doing?

Jana Defacing paintings.

Edwin I say, are you all right?

Jana Yes, of course, it's . . . it's just a shock to see this . . . suddenly.

Edwin Sorry, I should have warned you. . . . I . . .

Jana Don't be silly.

Edwin The gala opening's in Ottawa on Friday. You'll want to go, won't you? Might I have the honour, Ted, being fellow exiles and all, of escorting your wife to Ottawa for that event?

Ted What are you asking me for? She's right here.

Edwin Oh, do let's go to the gala. Lord knows, it's years, it'd be such fun. Good Lord, what an enormous bird. . . . Oh, right, that reminds me . . . I just popped in to see if there's anything I can pick up at the shops. I'm off to town. Now, you're not to worry about the drink, I'm getting that. We're going to have a real bang-up meal. . . .

Bear Cranberry sauce.

Edwin Good heavens, she's sewing it up with a needle and thread, like an old bag. How disgusting!

Bear Cranberry sauce.

Edwin What?

Bear Cranberry sauce. Ma always forgets cranberry sauce.

Edwin Right. Cranberry sauce. Anything else? Have we got a sweet?

Suza enters. She is wearing a pink nightgown

and fuzzy slippers and has a new, very radical haircut. She busies herself self-consciously, getting breakfast. Everyone is staring at her, speechless, except Jana, who is absorbed with what she is doing. Finally . . .

I say . . .

Jana looks up.

Jana Oh, my God!

Suza So?

Jana Are you crazy?

Suza I knew you'd say that, I just knew it.

Jana What the hell did you expect me to say? Very pretty? Have you gone completely out of your mind?

Suza I've thought about this very carefully. There's a principle involved here, *and I made an important decision.

Jana *This is some kind of solution? Think again, girl. It's not, it's absolutely not, it's for shit!

Suza *I thought perhaps you might be prepared to shut up and listen to what I have to say. *But I guess I was wrong.

Jana *I thought you were a smart girl, an intelligent girl, but you're not, you're just pigheaded and stupid.

Suza You never listen to me. Why don't you ever listen to me?

Jana Listen to you? Listen to you? All I have to do is look at you.

Edwin I think I'd better . . .

Edwin starts to slink out. Jana grabs him.

Jana Oh, no you don't. Look at her, look at her, your precious protégé, your Ontario scholar—so brilliant, so talented. She's been sent home three times this month alone for being improperly dressed at school, and now she goes and does this. This is partly your fault for . . .

Suza *It is not, this is *my* . . .

Jana . . . filling her head with elitist nonsense, thinking she's above the rules. She has to live in this community, get along with . . .

Suza You think I care about what . . .

Jana If you want to represent the county in the National High School debate, on national television, it will only be, on condition, *on condition,* you stick to the school dress code.

Suza An antiquated, sexist dress code that is the most demeaning, humiliating . . . I can't believe that you, my mother, *are supporting . . .

Jana *You think I give two potatoes how you or anybody else dresses themselves? That's not what this is about. This is about understanding priorities, knowing when to compromise.

Suza Oh, great! You want me to go on CBC television and debate the true meaning of western democracy dressed as a Barbie Doll.

Jana Grow up! You are going to lose it.

Suza Oh, come on, it's bluff, Mum, it's all bluff, they're not going to give it to . . .

Jana *Suzanna!

Suza *. . . someone else, there is no one else, they have to give it to me.

Jana They're going to call your bluff. You'll lose the debate, and you'll lose the scholarship.

Suza So I'll get a music scholarship later on.

Jana Oh, yes, the world is your oyster.

Suza You're not listening! We're talking about freedom here, Mum. There's a point that has to be made.

Jana What do you know about freedom, you with your sack full of choices? You know nothing about freedom.

Suza Well, then, why don't you give us the benefit of your sad East European past.

Edwin Suza, for God's sake!

Pause.

Jana So you could throw it in my face?

Pause.

The turkey goes in at twelve thirty at three hundred fifty degrees. I'm going fishing.

Jana grabs her jacket and tacklebox and exits.

Suza Fine!

Edwin Cranberry sauce . . . right.

Edwin exits.

Ted Think you better consider doing some fence mending on that one, Suza.

Silence.

You hear me?

Suza Why does she have to . . . ?

Ted I'm telling you!

Silence.

Suza?

Suza Yeh.

Ted *(to Bear)* Couple of guys coming in by noon for canoes. Don't forget to register them. Name a' Murphy or Moffit or some such.

Bear I won't.

Ted exits.

Pause.

Bear looks at Suza.

That what turns Gordie on?

Silence.

Cute . . . real cute.

SCENE THREE

Interior / exterior—baitshop and dock. Early afternoon.

When the door opens, a fluid light reflected onto the ceiling off the water in three bait tanks and off the lake outside. We hear Suza playing something lyrical on the violin. Bear is minding the store, drawing comics, doing sound effects aloud. The violon shifts into rock music for a while and eventually stops. The door creaks open.

Mirek Hallo?

Bear Oh, hi.

Mirek stands in the doorway.

Mirek I'm looking for Jana.

Bear Yah-na?

Mirek This is Jana's Landing, no?

Bear Oh, you mean Jan. She's gone fishing.

Mirek Ah.

Bear You wanna wait for her? You want some coffee?

Mirek Yes, please, I wait. Coffee, yes.

Mirek comes in.

Bear She always throws them back, but she goes anyway. Likes sitting there, I guess.

Mirek Oh, well, it sounds nice.

Bear Go ahead, coffee's right there.

Bear goes back to his comics. Mirek wanders over to the first bait tank and gazes in.

Mirek Frogs!

Bear Yeh.

Mirek moves to the second tank. Looks at Bear.

Minnows and crayfish, worms underneath. You going fishing?

Mirek I don't think so. Maybe. I've come to see Jana.

Bear You're a friend of hers, huh, friend of Ma's?

Mirek Yes, from long ago.

Bear puts his comics aside.

Bear You from . . . from Czechoslovakia?

Mirek Yes, that's right, from Prague. And you are?

Bear Blair. I'm Yah-na's son.

Mirek Ah, Jana's son, Blair. How do you do, Blair? I am Mirek.

They shake hands.

Bear You can call me Bear, everyone else does.

Mirek As in Polar Bear?

Bear No, as in Grizzly Bear.

Mirek Of course.

Bear Ma shouldn't be too long. . . . That is, usually she isn't, but then sometimes she goes all day. It sort of depends.

Mirek It is okay, I wait, I have no hurry.

Mirek takes out his camera, looks at stuff through it. He sniffs the air.

Mirek Mmmmmm.

Bear Turkey. You hit a good day. Guess you'll be staying for dinner, eh?

Mirek If I am invite. I hope.

Mirek plays with his camera, takes pictures, etc. Bear watches him.

Bear Were you, like, friends when you were kids or something?

Mirek Or something. We were lovers.

Bear Lovers! You and Ma were lovers? No kidding?

Mirek Forgive me. This is a shock for you?

Bear Oh . . . no, no, me and my friends, we talk about . . . well, what I mean is . . . we . . . I know about lovers. I have a girl friend, you know. We're not lovers, yet. I'm still a virgin, so far, but I imagine I'll have a lover sometime, sometime soon, probably.

Mirek Yes, I am sure. A lover is a wonderful thing to have.

Suza enters wearing a walkman and carrying a bucket and fish net. She glances at Mirek, then begins cleaning the tanks. Bear and Mirek watch.

Bear That's my sister.

Mirek Zuzanna.

Bear Yeh, right. How'd you know that?

Suza tears off the walkman.

Suza What'd you say?

Mirek Zuzanna. You look just like her.

Suza Who?

Mirek Your grandmother, Zuzanna.

Suza My grandmother? Who is this guy?

Bear This is Mirek, Suz, Ma's lover from the old days in Prague.

Suza You . . . you're who?

Mirek reaches out his hand.

Mirek Mirek, Mirek Sling. I've come from Europe to visit your mother. I'm an old friend.

Suza Oh . . . wow . . . does she know?

Mirek No, I . . . no, she doesn't.

Suza Gees, well, how about that, eh? Ah . . . welcome to Canada. Would you like some coffee? . . . No wait, it'll be stale. . . . I'll make . . .

Mirek Thank you, no.

Suza She's . . . um . . . Ma's gone fishing. . . . I don't know . . .

Bear Yeh, yeh, it's all under control. He's gonna wait.

Suza Right. . . . Well, then . . . I'll just . . .

Suza indicates what she's doing.

Mirek Oh, yes, please go on.

Pause.

Suza begins scooping crayfish out of the tank and shaking them into a bucket.

Suza Were you . . . were you and Mother in the . . . uh, Prague Spring together?

Mirek Yes, we were in the Prague Spring. I'm sorry, I am looking at you, it is very rude.

Suza Oh, it's okay, I don't mind.

Mirek takes out cigarettes, hesitantly offers one to Suza.

Yeh, sure.

Suza thrusts the fish net at Bear, who shrugs and takes over. Mirek lights Suza's cigarette.

Mirek I cannot believe it. I would know you anywhere. So amazing. Your name is really Zuzanna?

Suza Yeh, well, Susanne, I like Susanne better. So you knew my grandmother?

Mirek Yes. A very brilliant woman.

Suza She was a pianist, right?

Mirek A jazz pianist, a good one, and a journalist. We were together on a magazine in the sixties.

Bear Suza plays the violin.

Mirek Yes?

Bear She's real good.

Suza I'm okay.

Bear She won first prize in the Kiwanis Music Festival last year.

Suza Bear.

Bear She's gonna be famous, I bet.

Suza Bear!

Suza gives him a shove.

What d'you mean brilliant?

Mirek Zuzanna? She was fantastic. Everything she did. But she had a very hard life.

Suza In Prague.

Mirek Yes.

Suza I'm going to Prague some day.

Mirek Yes?

Suza I wanna study with Josef Suk.

Mirek So you are going to be famous.

Suza Yeh, right.

Bear Told ya.

Suza She died a long time ago, right? My grandmother?

Mirek In 1969, in the winter after the invasion. She died of a heart attack. She was asthma.

Suza She *had* asthma.

Mirek Yes. Had asthma.

Bear Uncle Otto said the communists broke her heart.

Mirek That's right, they did.

Bear And she looked like Suza?

Mirek Yes, except, not with this kind of hair.

Bear No kidding.

Suza Mum never talks about this stuff.

Mirek Stuff?

Bear Our grandparents, Prague.

Mirek But this is very bad. Why not?

Suza You'd have to ask her.

Bear All she ever talks about is going fishing with her Dad when she was little.

Mirek She always was a strange one, your mother.

Suza You can say that again.

Mirek She always was a strange one, your . . .

They crack up.

What?

Suza You can say that again. It's an expression, *it means . . .

Bear *It means, you're right. She's strange all right.

Mirek Oh, I see.

Suza What about our grandfather? He died when she was little, right?

Mirek No, not little. He came out of jail when she was sixteen already.

Bear *Jail?

Suza *Really?

Mirek Of course. He died after. You don't know these things?

Suza and Bear shake their heads.

He was political prisoner, victim of the Stalinist purges.

Bear Really?

Mirek Many people went to jail. Good people. Why doesn't she tell you these things?

Suza Who knows. I guess it's a secret.

Bear scoops the last of the bait and puts the bucket down with a clunk.

Mirek No more fishing, then?

Bear No, it's the end of the season . . . *(to Suza)* Hey, dork brain.

Bear gives Suza a shove.

Suza Okay, right. Great. Grab the other bucket.

Mirek Where do you put them?

Suza Dump them in the lake.

Suza and Bear go out onto the dock. Mirek follows.

Suza The frogs aren't so easy. Last time we cleaned tanks, Bear forgot to put the lid on the bucket and they got out. They got into the house, and we were catching them for days after. It was a riot.

Bear Dad stepped on one with his bare feet when he was going to the john in the middle of the night.

Suza and Bear empty the buckets into the lake.

Suza Mum just about died laughing.

Bear Dad was pissed as hell. You should'a seen him.

They laugh and return to the baitshop.

Mirek Your father. What is he? What does he do?

Bear *He's a physicist.

Suza *He's a businessman.

Suza and Bear look at each other.

Suza He runs the marina. He used to be a scientist.

Mirek A scientist. Mmmm.

Jana enters through the other door with a bucket, puts it on the table and examines its contents.

Bear Did you and Ma know each other when you were kids, or did you meet, like . . .

Mirek She was eighteen and I twenty. Your grandmother introduces us. It was very romantic.

Bear Yeh?

Mirek We were out in the country to interview an old man, a painter, but he was very . . . um . . . very . . . he didn't want to speak to us, so we went to a restaurant close by and your mother came to have lunch with us.

Jana takes a fish out of the bucket, then becomes aware of the voice in the other room.

Mirek It was in the springtime and very beautiful with flowers everywhere. This is the first time I saw her.

Bear *So?

Suza *And?

Mirek And I fell completely in love with her.

Suza *Go on.

Bear *And . . .

He laughs.

Mirek Okay. It was a funny thing. Zuzanna wanted very much to catch this painter, so she went away for a while, to "hatch a plot," leaving your mother and I to get to know each other.

Jana moves toward them.

When she came back, she had a big bag of clothes, and she dressed up your mother in a crazy costume, funny long dress, hat full of flowers, big red scarf and wings . . . wings

. . . like children wear in a play for school. It was very funny. Then back to the painter's house, and we hide in the bushes while your mother walks up and down in front, singing a little song—lalalala. Soon, the old man looks out of his window and then runs down to see if his old eyes are tricking him. We jumped out of the bushes, and that was how we got our interview.

Bear But wasn't he mad at you? I'd of been.

Mirek No. She was very clever, your grandmother. Jana was dressed exactly like a figure he had painted several times in his paintings, and he was delighted.

Suza What about the painter, why did you want to interview him?

Jana approaches, unobserved.

Mirek He was a wonderful painter but with no fingers. We wanted to know how he did it.

Bear No fingers? No kidding, how come?

Mirek It's hard to say what might have happened. He was a long time in jail in the fifties, like your grandfather.

Bear Why would they put a painter in jail?

Mirek He refused to paint what the communists wanted him to paint. He kept his own mind.

Suza How did he do it, with no fingers?

Mirek I don't know, we forgot to ask.

Bear That's easy. I know how they do that.

They notice Jana.

Suza Mum.

Mirek Jano!

Jana is holding the fish. Jana and Mirek stare at each other.

Pause.

Jana From underneath, in the dark, a fish, such a fish. . . . It has one eye only, and where the other should be, scales; silver, smooth as silk. And look, three fins. There should only be two. I have been . . . out . . . on the surface. The air is warm, the lake is winking, smooth, dreamy. . . . But underneath . . .

Jana and Mirek stand looking at each other. He takes the fish from her.

Mirek Here you are. You are here.

Jana touches Mirek's face.

Jana This face. The face of Mirek . . . Mirek Sling.

Mirek takes her hands, examines them, kisses them, looks in her eyes.

Mirek Jano . . . Jana Pavlova. Janicka

SCENE FOUR

Interior—living / dining room area. Evening.

Thanksgiving dinner is almost finished. Edwin is about to propose a toast. He is drunk. They are holding their glasses, suspended, waiting.

Silence.

Bear *Come on.

Suza *Edwin, my drink's evaporating.

Jana *We are waiting, Edwin.

Edwin Hang on, hang on, it's coming. . . . May the dissident souls and crusaders for the cultured life find continued safe refuge behind the stout shield of the Canadian wilderness.

They groan.

Suza Only slightly pompous, Edwin, only slightly.

Mirek Then you are a crusader, as you say, from where? England?

Edwin No! No, no. Ireland, my good man, the Emerald Isle.

Mirek Irish? But in my ear you are somebody in an English novel?

Jana has started to clear the plates. She remains busy until coffee and cognac.

Edwin Aha, that is a keen ear, my friend.

Jana Suza . . .

Suza It's Bear's turn.

Edwin What you are hearing is the product of English nannies, English boarding schools, English Imperialism, added to which, you could quite correctly call me a remittance man. . . .

Suza *Bear.

Mirek *A remittance man?

Edwin Unacceptable to my wealthy but neurotic family, I am sustained on a remittance, provided I remain in the outer reaches of the dominion.

Mirek Ah, a gentleman with a private income, yes?

Edwin *That's one way of putting it.

Suza *Bear! Clear the table!

Bear helps clear the the dishes around them. Edwim produces cigars, offers one to Mirek.

Mirek No, thank you.

Edwin lights one for himself.

Ted So, Mirek, when was it you left Czechoslovakia?

Mirek Two years ago.

Bear But if you and Ma were . . .

Bear glances at Ted.

I mean, how come you didn't leave when Ma did?

Mirek Because I was caught and put in prison.

Suza *Really?

Bear *You went to prison?

Mirek Yes, I did.

Bear How come?

Mirek I was caught trying to escape at a time when they didn't want people to escape.

Bear Wow!

Mirek takes out his cigarettes, offers one to Ted.

Ted Not for me.

Suza Yes, please.

Suza reaches for one.

Ted Suza!

Suza Just kidding.

Mirek lights one for himself.

Edwin The noblest and best minds of your generation sent down to rot.

Mirek That's right, a generation lost.

Edwin A toast, a toast. To the Velvet Revolution. To the Poet King.

Mirek To Mr. Havel.

Edwin To Mr. Havel.

They raise their glasses.

Mirek And you, Mr. Potts, what is it a remittance man is doing in the outer reaches of the dominion?

Edwin Carrying on the lofty tradition of drunken Irish poet.

Mirek Poet?

Suza Well, drunken anyway. Our very own living, breathing, Irish stereotype.

Edwin glares at her.

Edwin Actually, no, I embellish the truth. Strictly speaking, I'm a memoirist.

Suza guffaws.

Suza A memoirist!?

Mirek So you are writing. What are you writing?

Edwin A memoir, Mr. Sling, of a very personal nature.

Suza A memoir of a personal nature. Well, that's original. How about a synopsis, Edwin. Hey, "Synopsis and Cognac." Now there's a . . .

Edwin Eh?

Suza "Synopsis and Cognac."

Edwin No, no, my dear, but . . . "Synopsis of the Soul."

Suza Ooh, fab. "Synopsis of the Soul." Yeh!

Edwin Yes . . . "Synopsis of the Soul!" Yes, I like that.

Suza Well, at least you have a title, eh?

Suza giggles.

Edwin Ah, the cruelty of children, Mr. Sling. No respect for their elders.

Ted Don't mind her. She quit believing anything adults say ages ago.

Bear Dad, Suza's had too much wine.

Ted whips Suza's glass away.

Ted And what do you do in Paris, Mirek? You live in Paris now, right?

Mirek Yes, at the moment. I am owner, with one other, of a small gallery. Also, I am becoming, slowly . . . I don't know how you call it . . . agent? . . . representative? . . . for some artists in Czechoslovakia and one or two in other countries in Central Europe also.

Ted Great. That must be real interesting. Make much money at it?

Mirek Of course not.

Ted And these photos that are going to Ottawa?

Mirek Yes?

Ted They come from this gallery you got in Paris.

Mirek It's my exhibition, yes, I put it together.

Ted So they're your photos?

Mirek Mostly, yes, but other people also . . . and I am here also to sniff in this country. I am going to stay for a while in Montreal and Toronto and then New York after.

Ted Great.

Edwin Jan, darling, I'd like to propose another toast. . . . To Mirek, for putting a new sparkle into Jan's eyes.

They groan.

Suza Oh, Edwin, tacky-tacky.

Mirek It is so beautiful, this place, Ted.

Ted Yeh.

Mirek Do you own the whole lake?

Ted Nope. Six acres, the marina, eight cabins and the trailer park. Yep, a good little business for the most part.

Edwin And the most ideal writer's retreat through the long winter months.

Jana enters with a tray of empty cups.

Jana Coffee.

Edwin That was a superlative meal, Jan. You've really outdone yourself.

Jana sets down the tray and exits to fetch the coffee. Ted places the brandy tray in front of Edwin.

Ah!

Edwin proceeds to open the bottle and pour.

Suza Why did you want to escape?

Mirek Because life in Czechoslovakia was . . . had become . . . horrible. We wanted to live in the West.

Suza We?

Mirek Your mother and I. Many people.

Bear Wow! No kidding!

Edwin hands round the cognac. Jana enters and pours coffee from a large espresso maker.

Bear *Like, did you escape like . . . how did . . .

Edwin *And now, the coup de gras . . .

Edwin raises his glass.

To the exhibition. May it have no unforeseen consequences.

Ted What the hell's that supposed to mean?

Edwin *I haven't the foggiest idea.

Bear *What do you mean "escape"? Did Ma escape?

Mirek But of course your mother escaped.

Bear Well, like how?

Mirek She escaped on bus. I was hanging under a train.

Suza Hanging under a train?

Bear Like, what do you mean?

Mirek Well, "like," hanging on, you know, with your hands. We were . . .

Mirek looks at Jana.

Mam o tom mluvit . . . ? *(You don't mind . . . ?)*

Jana Klidne muzes. *(No, it's all right.)*

Mirek We were visiting friends on the Austrian border. Jana went on a tour bus across the border to see an exhibition. If we went together, the authorities would know we would not come back, so some friends took me to a place where I could get under the train, showed me how to hold on.

Suza Under the train?

Mirek Yes, there are places. It is not too difficult, for a short distance. But they discovered me at the border, put me in a van and took me back to Prague. It was the last time we saw each other.

Bear No kidding.

Suza So, what did you do Mum?

Jana I went to our rendezvous. That was Vienna.

Suza You didn't go back for him?

Jana After four days I knew he didn't make it, so I went to London, stayed with friends as we had planned.

Suza God! Then what happened?

Jana I waited. After six months, he was sentenced, Mirek and four others.

Bear What did you get sentenced to?

Mirek Three years . . . at that time.

Suza *(to Ted)* Did you know all this?

Ted Yes.

Suza *(to Jana)* How come you never told us?

Jana You never asked, I guess.

Bear Then Uncle Otto came to London, right? And you were real sick, and he brought you home . . . to Canada, I mean. That part I know.

Suza Piss me off!

Jana Suza!

Suza Why don't I know all this stuff?

Jana I didn't know you didn't know. It wouldn't occur to me to just tell you out of the blue. It's all history. Anyway, it doesn't matter. More coffee, Edwin?

Edwin You're a dark horse, Jana Pavlova, a dark horse.

Suza That's my mother, all right, pitch black.

Mirek And you, Mr. Edwin Potts, memoirist, you are an "odd fish," yes?

Edwin Good. Good. Le mot juste! And in English no less. Yes, an odd fish I may be, Mr. Sling, but I'm in good company, believe me.

Bear Yeh, he's tanked.

Edwin Soggy, that's all, just a trifle soggy. That's why God invented whiskey, don't you know, to keep the Irish from conquering the world.

Edwin pours another round.

Suza You were a political prisoner, right?

Mirek Yes.

Suza If Mum had been caught, she would have been a political prisoner, too, right?

Mirek Yes.

Suza What were you doing that would make you a political prisoner?

Jana Subversive activities.

Suza What?

Jana Agitating. Organizing. Shooting off my mouth.

Suza But what? Gees, getting information out of you's like . . .

Jana We were part of the cultural underground—having private exhibitions, reading plays in people's houses, typing and distributing manuscripts, all sorts of things.

Bear And just for doing that you could have been a political prisoner?

Mirek Basically, yes.

Suza Then what happened? Why did you have to leave all of a sudden?

Jana We began to see that things were not going to change. Life became unbearable. We wanted a new life, we wanted to have . . .

Jana shrugs.

Suza What?

Jana We wanted to have a new life. It doesn't matter anymore, it's all in the past.

Jana pours more coffee and wine.

Suza *(to Mirek)* See what I mean?

Jana What?

Suza It's all a closely guarded secret. I learned more about my grandparents from you in ten minutes than in the whole rest of my life.

Jana Suza, please. It makes me uncomfortable, that's all. My life is here, now, in Canada.

Suza Huh, some life. . . .

Suza does a "Garbo."

Suza "I vant to be alone. . . . I'm going feeshing."

Jana Look, you think it's all a big game, like a KGB spy novel, but it's not, it's my life. Has it ever occurred to you that perhaps it might be too painful for me to have to . . . to . . .

Edwin There once was a lady of cultyah,
A brilliant Bohemian sculptah,
Though her talent was ripping,
Her history gripping,
Her offspring were greedy wee vultyahs.

Laughter.

Ted So you left Prague two years ago. Why was that?

Mirek The photographs made me leave. I used to keep them in my father's potato cellar. He lived on a farm. When he died, I lost my hiding place and when you have been in jail in my country you become very . . . very . . .

Mirek looks at Jana.

Jana Paranoid.

Mirek Yes, for my pictures I was paranoid, and it was very dangerous. It is a very important collection, and it was essential that I get them out.

Ted And it's pictures of . . . of pictures . . . art.

Jana Oh, for . . .

Mirek Yes, sculpture, painting, drawings, exhibitions.

Ted And Jan's art? Her big statues and that?

Edwin Sculpture, Ted, please, they're sculptures.

Mirek Of course. Her work is one of the main features of the exhibition.

Bear *No kidding?

Ted *Well, ain't that something. A main feature, eh, Jan?

Mirek I came all this way to finally get her permission, a little late perhaps, but I hope she will forgive me, and to pay her, of course . . . *(to Jana)* and to bring you to Ottawa for the opening, if you will, Jana.

Silence.

It would be a great honour . . . for us.

Silence.

Suza And you're going to pay her?

Mirek Of course I'm going to pay her. She's a professional artist.

Bear She is?

Mirek But . . . of course she is.

Suza So where's the photographs?

Ted Yeh, you got the pictures with you? Let's see them. You're gonna be a celebrity, Jan. How about that, eh?

Mirek Jana?

Jana You have . . . "Bez Omezeni." *(Without Limitations.)*

Mirek nods.

You have . . .

Mirek I have everything.

Jana "Palach"?

Mirek Especially "Palach."

Pause.

Ted Come on. Let's see them.

Jana No.

Edwin Easy does it there, Ted.

Ted *Sure. Why not? Where are they, Mirek?

Bear *I didn't know you were famous, Ma.

Jana *No!*

Ted Why?

Jana Because it's private, and it's . . . it's . . .

Edwin An artist's prerogative.

Suza What's the big deal? *It's just us.

Jana *It is a big deal. It's a huge deal. You know nothing about it.

Edwin *Hands off, hands off the artist's soul! These aren't family snapshots. These are the missing chunks of the woman's very soul, her lost children come home.

Jana Thank you Edwin.

Edwin Pearls before bloody swine.

Jana Edwin! I will look at them by myself, later. Then, if I feel comfortable, I will show them to you.

Jana leaves the room.

Suza God!

Bear What's "Palash" . . . whatever . . . and that other thing you said?

Mirek Jan Palach was a student who burned himself to death, as a protest, six months after the Soviet invasion. Jana did a memorial to him, a large sculpture. It was defaced, then confiscated. "Bez Omezeni" was the piece that won her the European Sculpture Prize in the spring of '68.

Everyone looks stunned.

Bear Wow!

Mirek You don't know these things?

Silence.

Bear shakes his head.

Mirek I . . . I don't understand. . . . She isn't . . . she doesn't . . . ?

Edwin No, old chap, she doesn't.

Pause.

Mirek I see. Your mother was one of Czechoslovakia's most controversial and important young artists.

Ted She never talks about it.

Edwin She's a brilliant talent, wasted, wasted. I've always known it.

Ted She used to draw all the time, back in the early days. Then she just kinda stopped. Got too busy, I guess.

Suza It's a secret part of her she likes to keep from us. She hoards it to herself.

Ted Now, Suz, that ain't fair.

Suza It's true.

Bear It hurts her.

Edwin If the Good Lord had intended our every thought and memory to be viewed by the world, he would have given us goldfish bowls instead of heads.

Jana reenters.

Jana Edwin, you're drunk.

Edwin The pain and vulnerability of the artist is incomprehensible to the plebeian world under the best of circumstances, but you put Stalin into the equation and . . .

Jana Oh, for God's sake, Edwin, do shutup. You talk the most awful garbage sometimes.

The phone rings as Edwin staggers to his feet.

Suza *Oh, that'll be Gord. I'll get it.

She dashes out.

Edwin *Picture a pair of big, beautiful pearly gates. Mr. Brezhenv is standing outside, begging to be allowed in. Mr. Kosygin is standing inside, shouting, "No, for God's sake, don't come in!" "But why not?" cries Brezhenv, "This is heaven." "That's what I thought," says Kosygin, "but the bloody Czechs have switched all the street signs!"

Jana, Mirek and Ted burst out laughing.

I've been around, you know, I've been around.

Edwin wobbles dangerously. Ted catches him.

Edwin Much obliged. I think per'aps . . .

Ted 'Bout time for bed, ol' buddy, ol' pal?

Edwin Heave to. Good night, good night.

They struggle out the back door.

Soviet paralysis, the most progressive paralysis in the world.

Bear He's so cute, isn't he?

Edwin Top o' the evening to ye!

Silence.

Jana And that's Thanksgiving dinner, Canadian style.

Mirek Does it always end so quickly?

Jana Only if Edwin's here, and look, he's forgotten his jacket.

Bear grabs his jacket and runs off with it.

Bear Gees, what a no-brain.

Mirek pushes his glass forward. Jana pours.

Silence.

Mirek I like your children.

Jana Thank you, they're good kids.

Mirek Very bright.

Jana Suza plays the violin.

Mirek Yes, she told me.

Jana She's very good. We have been lucky to have a wonderful teacher for her near here, but he is leaving. I don't know what we'll do.

Silence.

Here we are. How do you like Canada?

They laugh.

Mirek It's beautiful, thank you, everybody is very nice.

Pause.

Jana *Where do we start?

Mirek *You are so different.

They laugh.

You have changed.

Jana No, it's not possible.

Mirek Yes, just a little bit. You are . . .

Jana Twenty years older.

Mirek Of course, but . . . softer, smoother, something.

Jana Softer?

Mirek Yes, around the edges, there's something . . .

Jana Motherhood.

Mirek Maybe.

Silence.

You are more beautiful.

Jana Oh don't, please.

Mirek You are angry.

Jana My life has fallen in two halves. I never thought to see them come together.

Mirek And you are angry.

Jana I . . . I am in shock.

Mirek I should have warned you. I'm sorry.

Jana No. I . . .

Mirek I have thought of this moment for so long. You cannot imagine the scenes I have had in my head.

Jana Yes, I can. I did that, too. For years.

Mirek reaches across the table.

Mirek Why did you . . .

Bear enters and sits down.

Bear Boy, is he drunk.

Silence.

Right . . . I think I hear my mother calling.

Bear exits.

Mirek What?

Jana A silly joke.

Mirek That one is certainly not very bright, and no sense of humour.

Jana He makes comic books. He makes up the story, draws the pictures.

Mirek And makes all the noises also. I heard him.

Jana They're very funny. And very, very clever.

Pause.

Mirek It is nineteen years, five months and four days.

Jana Exactly?

Mirek Exactly. Tell me about your life.

Jana I am what you see. I run a business, I look after a family.

Mirek Yes?

Jana That's a lot. You don't know.

Mirek Yes, no doubt. And you were out in a canoe, fishing, when I arrived. An idyllic Canadian dream. Is it truly possible?

Jana I suppose.

Mirek And you are totally happy?

Jana It's a real life, Mirek, not a fantasy.

Mirek You are not making art.

Jana No.

Pause.

Mirek Why?

Jana In ten words or less?

Mirek Why don't you have a studio in the woods? It's perfect.

Jana You think it's so simple?

Mirek It's not?

Jana No.

Mirek But it's very sad.

Jana pours more wine.

Jana Maybe.

Mirek Maybe? Of course it's sad. It's a huge waste.

Jana My life is different now.

Mirek But you are the same person.

Jana Maybe. Maybe not. It takes a long time to know who you are in a new country. As an immigrant, you have to remake yourself. At least I did.

Mirek And you have no regrets?

Jana Of course I have regrets, but I have learned to live with them. I have had to make choices.

Mirek Choices?

Jana Stop it. Tell me about you. When did your father die?

Mirek Nineteen eighty-seven. And you made a choice to leave out the creative part when you remade yourself?

Jana Yes! I guess I did!

Mirek No. No. I may not know the new Jan you have so carefully made of yourself, Janicko, but I do know the creative drive that is fundamental to your personality. You can't change that much. . . .

Jana What is this? An interrogation?

Mirek It can't simply be eliminated. It's not a habit, like smoking. . . .

Jana What makes you think you have the right to come in here and judge my decisions.

Mirek You can't just *lose* it.

Jana Stop it! You know nothing about what it means to . . .

Mirek How can this be a good life, if you, Jana Pavlova, are not expressing yourself?

Pause.

Jana Why did you come here?

Mirek What do you think? I came to tell you about my years in prison?

Jana Ah.

Mirek Don't be silly.

Jana Oh, yes, I think so.

Mirek I came to find out what can keep Czechoslovakia's most promising and talented sculptor from working.

Jana You are a shit, you know that? You haven't changed a bit.

Mirek You have, your bum's bigger.

Jana So is your nose.

Mirek That's what keeps me in business.

Jana All right!

Jana pours more wine.

Jana Contrary to what you seem to think, when you leave your country, your whole life, your friends, your culture, everything and go to a . . . a new everything, you can't simply start being an artist again, just like that, poof! It doesn't work that way.

Mirek But in twenty years . . .

Jana Canada is not what you think. To be an artist in Canada, it's . . . it's . . . well. There are many different ways in which artists are silenced.

Mirek Of course, but I'm not talking about Canada, I'm . . .

Jana There is no understanding here, no love, no dignity. In Canada, art is considered unnecessary.

Mirek Oh, come on, art is how people speak to each other. There are theatres here, concerts, paintings. People write books here.

Jana But it has no roots, it doesn't come from the forest floor. It's imported, disconnected. Canada doesn't want artists.

Mirek Ah, so you are without a cause? Is that what you mean?

Jana Mirku, miles and miles and miles of Canada out there that think poets and sculptors are something out of story books . . . story books written in Europe. This country is asleep.

Mirek And this is why you don't work?

Jana Yes. No. It's that . . . I . . . I

Mirek What?

Jana I don't know. . . . I . . . I couldn't find the pieces.

Mirek The pieces?

Jana Yes . . . of . . . of the puzzle. I couldn't find a home, a . . . a place to feel whole.

Mirek But you of all people should be able to deal with compromised circumstances. Art thrives in compromised circumstances.

Jana Oh, for God's sake, it's different. You cannot thrive in a vacuum, you need a community that will . . .

Mirek Those are the circumstances with which you work, Jano.

Jana You cannot dictate to me what circumstances are right for me as an artist. You can't do that.

Mirek But this is your cause, if you need a cause. I don't understand what is your problem, Jano.

Jana Too bad! I'm not accountable to you! I could be a potato farmer if I wanted to. Maybe I don't *want* to be an artist anymore.

Mirek No. Not possible.

Jana You have no right to come in here and dig around and disturb my life!

Mirek I'm not.

Jana Yes, you are. This is my life. Leave it alone.

Mirek I spent twenty years telling myself that you were free; free of the lies, the silence, the internal death, free to work and create and make great art.

Jana And my life is supposed to justify your life, what fate has done to you? This is sick!

Mirek You don't know what it means to be in a communist jail and have the one comfort, the one light at the end of the tunnel extinguished.

Jana This is why you came here, to accuse me of betraying you.

Mirek Why did you stop writing to me?

Jana But it was you who stopped writing to me!

Mirek In London, you didn't write to me for weeks and weeks.

Jana I couldn't. I was ill, very ill. But later, I . . .

Mirek Did you have a lover in London, too?

Jana No! No! How could you? I wanted to die when you were sentenced. I wanted to go back, and I became very ill.

Mirek You abandoned me, you betrayed me. . . .

Jana No, I . . . you . . .

Mirek Men go insane for that. Men commit suicide for that.

Jana You think I don't know that? You think I haven't carried that through all the years? It made me very ill. But you think your suffering is the only suffering there is. You don't know what it was like for us, who got out, for me.

Mirek No. How could I? I stayed. I was five years in jail.

Jana Oh, yes, the great martyr. My life *is* supposed to justify your life, and here I am not making great art. How dare I? Five long years in jail and not one sculpture to show for it. Poor Mirek. I'm sorry about your years in jail, you will never know how sorry, but my life belongs to me now. You cannot come in here demanding to know what I'm doing as if I'm your invention, your property. There is no more sculpture, Mirek. Listen carefully: it's over, it's finished, it's gone.

Jana breaks down.

Pause.

Mirek I'm sorry. When I saw your perfect life, with your perfect children and your perfect husband, I . . . I . . . the years of loneliness . . . I'm sorry, Janicko. I didn't mean to hurt you.

Pause.

Jana I thought you married.

Mirek I did. It didn't work. We divorced after four years.

Pause.

Jana Oh, Mirku, we are still fighting. We would never have made it.

Mirek My wife and I never fought.

Jana I fight, Ted doesn't.

Pause.

Mirek When is the last time you went to a gallery, saw an exhibition?

Jana I don't remember, two, three years ago.

Mirek Janicko, creativity doesn't simply go away. It's not like a bucket of water that can be emptied.

Jana Mirku, please.

The moon comes out. Jana notices, goes to the window and looks at it.

Full moon. You should go up north, farther north. Ted's mother comes from the north. It's wonderful, you cannot imagine . . . trees and rocks and lakes that go on and on and on. I stood quietly in that ancient forest, a bruised Czech refugee, trying to find out who I was, where I belonged. There was a great hole in my middle, a great aching hole, shaped like you and my mother and my friends and my home and my past, everything . . . all those things that tell you who you are and how to speak to the world.

Mirek Yes.

Jana Then there was this place, so clean and soothing. I would go in a canoe out onto the lake and just sit for hours. A refuge. And then there was Ted, a whole new universe waiting to be tasted and willing to love, simply, without question. And, of course, the children, who filled me and made my life real, very real.

Pause.

Mirek And the hole? What of the hole?

Jana As they grow and find their own lives and fight their own struggles, I . . .

She looks at the moon.

The faceless ones . . . Do you know what I learned, listening in the great northern forests? It takes thousands and thousands of years to belong. The soul of this land is not ours, us Europeans, we are still strangers here. The heart, the soul of this country belongs only to its own people. Oh, yes, I am still Czech . . . but the artist . . . ?

Jana shrugs. Ted enters and stands silently at the back.

Mirek Come with me to Ottawa.

Jana I don't think so.

Mirek Please, tomorrow. Come with me.

Jana I'll have a hangover.

Mirek It doesn't matter. We'll go to galleries, concerts, the theatre. We'll see Henry Moore and Michael Snow. Oh, Jano, when I've missed you, and I do still miss you, I miss you most in galleries, looking at exhibitions.

He touches her face.

Nobody looks the way you do, even when you're drunk.

Jana laughs at him.

Jana Now who's drunk. What a silly old fool!

Mirek Yes. Come with me.

Jana and Mirek clasp hands and stand head to head swaying. Finally, Mirek breaks away, fetches the portfolio.

Come, it's time to look.

Ted bangs the door and comes in.

Ted. Did you put Edwin into bed?

Ted Yip, pretty routine round here. . . . Full moon out there, feels like September.

Ted puts his hand possessively on Jana's shoulder.

Mirek Yes, it's very beautiful. We were looking at it.

Ted These the pictures?

Mirek Yes.

Ted So?

Mirek I think perhaps . . . if you don't mind . . . Good night. I'm going to bed. Thank you for dinner.

Jana You don't need . . . ?

Mirek No, no, stay.

Mirek exits.

Ted So?

Jana This is something I have to do alone, d'you understand?

Ted I guess.

Jana I'll be there soon.

Ted Sure.

Ted starts to exit.

Jana Ted?

Ted stops.

Why do you do that?

Ted What?

Jana Put on that act.

Ted I don't know what you're talking about.

Jana Yes, you do; behave like a county bum.

Ted It's country bumpkin, and you're imagining things.

Jana And you're lying.

Pause.

I want to go with Mirek to Ottawa.

Ted Yeh, I figured.

Jana How do you feel about it?

Ted Doesn't matter, does it?

Jana Of course it matters.

Ted Why? Would it change anything?

Jana I don't know. Maybe.

Ted I figure you gotta do what you gotta do.

Jana Yes, but I want to know . . .

Ted You're a grown woman, Jan, you can do what you like.

Jana I'm not asking your permission.

Ted Then what are you asking?

Jana I want to know how you feel about me going away with my ex-lover to look at my ex-life.

Ted I feel fine. Can I go to bed now?

Jana Yes.

Ted starts to exit.

Ted.

Ted stops, remains with his back to her.

I love you.

Ted Oh, Jan, life's a bitch and then you die.

Jana Goddamnit, why do you say that? I hate it.

Ted Yeh, well . . .

Ted exits.

Pause.

Jana turns to the portfolio, empties the last of the wine into her glass, sips, puts it down, then slowly opens the portfolio and looks at the first picture. Lights fade to black.

fin.

ACT TWO SCENE ONE

Interior of Miller home. Early morning.

Bear is eating. Ted is making lunches.

Bear You remember to get fruit?

Ted Nope.

Bear Granola bars?

Ted Couldn't find them. Got cookies.

Bear Boy!

Ted Ma'll be back today.

Bear Bets?

Ted She said she will, and she will.

Bear Dad, there's two feet of snow out there, the roads'll be a mess.

Ted She'll be here.

Bear Don't give me bologna, I hate bologna.

Ted Picky, picky. So what do you want, cheese?

Bear Yeh, anything. One cheese, one peanut butter. D'you know where my boots are?

Ted Suze can have the bologna.

Bear You're the only one likes bologna, Dad.

Ted *(shouting off)* Suza! It's ten to seven. . . . Get up!

Bear She's in the shower.

Ted What's eating you this morning?

Bear Nothing. I don't like it with Ma away. I wish it didn't snow.

Ted I know, me, too. It's okay, she'll be back.

Silence.

Bear eats. Ted finishes lunches.

How's your project?

Bear Which one?

Ted Science.

Bear Environmental Studies.

Ted Whatever.

Pause.

So?

Bear Great.

Pause.

Ted So?

Bear It's called "Chewed Leaves and Caterpillar Poop." Great title, eh?

Ted Caterpillar poop?

Bear Yeh, you know, that yuech green slime they leave all over the deck for weeks.

Ted Well, it's different, that's for sure. What happened to "Captain PCB"?

Bear does a thumbs down.

Wouldn't go for it, eh?

Bear No imagination.

Ted Too bad. What's this one about?

Bear It's a theory I've got. You know how bad the caterpillars have been the last couple of years and how many trees we've lost?

Ted Yeh.

Bear Well, my theory is that it's like lemmings, only it's like a suicide pact between the trees and the caterpillars. . . . No really, Dad, you see, with acid rain being so bad and what with the PCBs and pollution and all, it's getting to be so there isn't enough air to go around so the trees kind of work out this deal with the bugs, right? It's sort of like tree depression. . . .

Ted Tree depression?

Bear Well, despair. You know, with the natural world going to rat shit. . . .

Ted Bear, nature's thrust is towards life and regeneration, not death and extinction.

Bear I know. So why do the lemmings rush to their deaths then?

Ted That's an old wives' tale, Bear.

Bear Oh, is it?

Ted Of course, it's just a migration where some of them end up getting drowned.

Bear Oh, I thought maybe the trees could be doing the same thing, with the environment being such a mess and all.

Ted Sounds a bit far-fetched to me. Have you done any research?

Bear It's not due till Christmas.

Ted Right. *Suza!* You're gonna miss the bus!

Suza *(from off)* Gord's got the car.

Ted What's she doing in there?

Bear digs around in a closet, looking for boots.

Bear They got the final debate at lunchtime, then after, the principal's gonna announce who's going to the National. Gotta do herself up, y'know, make her point.

Ted Have you tried the basement?

Bear Oh, yeh.

He exits as Suza enters with her violin, done up in her most radical best.

Ted Holy bejesus, you belong in a cage at the zoo.

Suza Gee thanks, Dad, you look swell, too.

Ted Are you aware there's two feet of snow out there?

Suza So?

Suza attends to breakfast. A pair of boots is thrown in to the room.

Bear *(shouting from off)* Dad! You want yours?

Ted Yeh, sure.

Another pair of boots is tossed in. Suza glances out the window.

Suza Well, shit!

Ted What?

Suza There's two feet of snow out there.

Ted looks at her.

How's Gord gonna get in?

Ted Got me.

Suza This is awful.

Ted Radical.

Suza Dad, please.

Ted What's he driving?

Suza His Mum's Toyota.

Ted He's not.

Suza Well . . . aren't you gonna plow out the road?

Ted Maybe.

Suza Maybe . . . what do you mean, maybe?

Ted If it hasn't warmed up and melted by the time I get the plow hooked up, I'll plow out the road.

Bear reenters and drops a pair of boots at Suza's feet.

Suza Ooooh, get them away from me. They'd probably give me warts or halitosis or something.

Bear You're right, they are definitely diseased.

Suza How long does it take to hook up the plow?

Ted Depends.

Suza Dad!

Ted Anywhere between one hour and all day.

Suza Dad!

Bear Face it, Suz, you're gonna have to walk to the highway, and you're gonna have to wear *those.*

Suza No way.

Ted Have you run this caterpillar business by your teacher yet?

Bear No.

Ted This is a science project, right?

Bear Yeh, but I can have a theory and either prove it or disprove it, right?

Ted Yeh.

Bear So what's the problem?

Ted Well, you have to be able to come up with some evidence to support a theory.

Bear I know it's a bit far-fetched, but that's okay, it's the product of an original mind.

Suza Is that what you call it?

Bear Who asked you?

Suza Science? Out of that mind?

Ted It does sound a bit more like science fiction.

Bear Yeh . . . maybe. Hey now, that's not a bad idea.

Ted You know, there's good evidence around to suggest that trees have some quite sophisticated ways of protecting themselves against attacks by bugs.

Bear Like what?

Ted Like producing protective chemicals—tannins, alkaloids, which the bugs don't like.

Bear No kidding?

Ted Not only that, but they have some kind of telegraph method of letting other trees know what's coming so they can be ready.

Suza Yeh, I've seen that happen, whole forests running like hell in the other direction.

Bear Yeh, right, science out of that brain? Okay, Dad, then how come so many trees have died the last couple of years?

Ted Could simply be a process of natural selection, pruning. With all due respect to man's atrocious impact on the environment, death is a natural process of the natural world, you know.

Bear Hmmmmm. That's not bad, Swami, not bad at all.

Ted Gee thanks, Bear. You're not going to find it in the school library, though.

Bear Yeh, well, Ma was gonna take me in to the Trent library.

Ted So? she'll be back . . . today probably.

Bear Yeh, right.

Suza I'm not gonna hold my breath.

She exits to basement. An urgent banging is heard at the door.

Ted Who the hell's that at this hour? I'm comin', I'm comin'!

He exits to the door.

Edwin The radio, quick, it's Jan on the radio!

Edwin dashes in wearing a parka and pajama bottoms, runs to the radio and turns it on.

Bloody hell . . . it's Jan . . . and Mirek . . . FM, FM, where's the knob for FM? *CBC FM? Where is it?

Bear *Ma's on the radio? . . . Suza! Ma's on the radio!

Suza reenters with a pair of heavy gardening boots. She drops the boots, goes to the radio and finds the station. During the interview, Suza and Bear get ready to go—finding coats, hats, packing lunches, books, etc.—steady, slow biz, giving the audience something to look at without distracting from the interview. Ted and Edwin concentrate fully on the radio.

A burst of laughter, then:

Jana . . . ghosts, like seeing ghosts.

CBC Yes, of course, it must be an extraordinary déjà vu. Now, tell us about this underground artist's colony that produced all this work.

Jana We were just friends mostly and colleagues, artist of various kinds who were continuing to do their own work after the invasion.

Mirek Refusing to be dictated to by the regime. And not just visual artists, but performing artists as well. Musicians, actors and writers.

CBC And the consequences were?

Mirek It meant going underground, never having public showings, exhibitions, performances.

Jana Our audience became only our close friends.

CBC I see. Jana, your own work is marvelous, astonishing, even now. It must have been quite breathtaking in the flesh . . . er, clay.

Jana Stone . . . mostly.

CBC Stone.

Jana Yes. Thank you.

CBC And every piece was destroyed?

Mirek Yes, all her major work. The authorities broke into a private exhibition and destroyed it.

CBC How tragic.

Jana Yes.

CBC Could you tell us about that incident?

Pause.

Mirek Jana?

Pause.

Jana It was a private exhibition, you understand.

CBC Yes?

Jana In a barn . . . the work of about half a dozen young and very talented artists. It hadn't opened yet. We were preparing an opening reception.

Mirek Which was to include . . .

Jana Yes, it was to include a performance of a new mime piece by a group of actors, together with some newly composed music.

Mirek All of it important, innovative, new work.

Jana We had spent about two days getting it ready, and . . . on the afternoon . . . it was . . . someone tipped off the authorities.

CBC Yes?

Mirek Four young firemen were sent out to dismantle it.

CBC Firemen?

Mirek Yes, communist bureaucracy works in very strange ways.

CBC Firemen. And they destroyed everything?

Mirek Yes.

CBC And you witnessed this, did you not, Jana?

Mirek Yes, she did. . . .

Edwin Good Lord!

Jana I was there alone at the time. I was hidden in the hay loft.

CBC It must have been excruciating.

Jana Of course. It's with you for the rest of your life.

Pause.

CBC Thank you for sharing this with us.

Jana You're welcome.

CBC And thank you both for joining me this morning.

Both Thank you.

CBC That exhibition, entitled "Lost Voices," can be seen at the Smythe Lee Gallery on Sparks Street till the end of the month . . . definitely not to be missed.

Music. Ted turns it down.

Pause.

Bear Why'd you let her go! She's never gonna come back now! You shouldn't have let her go! Why'd you let her go!

Ted What'd you want me to do? Lock her in her room?

Bear I don't care, you shouldn't have let her go!

Ted Hey Bear, it's okay, she'll be back.

Bear Oh, sure, what do you know!

He exits, slamming the door. Suza is ready to go but sitting, not moving.

Suza Did you know about that . . . that stuff in the barn?

Ted No.

Suza *(to Edwin)* Did you?

Edwin shakes his head.

How come she never told us?

Ted I dunno, Suz. There's probably a lot of stuff we don't know. Don't be angry with her. Something like that must be real painful.

Pause.

Those are Mum's gardening boots.

Suza So?

Pause.

She's sleeping with him, you know. I just know she's sleeping with him. Don't you care?

Pause.

She exits. Edwin and Ted sit unmoving.

Silence.

Ted She gonna come home, Edwin?

Edwin This tragic, tragic burden, and we never knew.

Ted Tragic burden, my ass! Why the hell don't I know these things?

Edwin Good question.

Ted Goddamm it! Why wouldn't she tell me?

Edwin The mysterious, romantic woman. Perhaps you wanted to keep her that way.

Ted That's bullshit!

Edwin I always knew there was something very dark, something she was burying.

Ted And how is it you always seem to know so much more about her than the rest of us.

Edwin Because I'm a damned nosy parker, that's why. I stick my big Irish nose in, and I ask questions.

Ted Okay then, if she's such a bloody big talent what in the hell is she doing here, with me, running a two-bit business in the middle of nowhere?

Edwin Another good question. And what about you?

Ted What about me?

Edwin Why are you here, in the middle of nowhere?

Ted What's that got to do with it?

Edwin Go on, why are you here?

Ted Because scientific research drove me up the wall. Who the hell cares?

Edwin What's the real reason?

Ted That is the real goddamn reason. What are you getting at?

Edwin You were wondering why you've lived with a woman for twenty years and don't know her. Am I right?

Ted Yeh, that's right, I'm wondering.

Edwin Fine. This is what I think. Number one, you didn't ask. Number two, she has a lot of pain and suffering buried deep inside that she hasn't been able to unload.

Ted Obviously.

Edwin I would guess because she hasn't felt safe enough, secure enough, to unload.

Ted And what the hell am I? Chopped liver?

Edwin Of course, as her husband you would like to think . . .

Ted That's right, I'm her husband with the right to . . .

Edwin That's right, shout at me, but I do know what I'm talking about.

Ted How come you're the expert?

Edwin Because you can't nurse the only person you've ever loved through three years of a bloody awful cancer without learning a thing or two about loving relationships.

Ted Okay. Sorry.

Edwin The fact is, you haven't a hope in hell of getting very far beneath the surface unless you're prepared to be honest with yourself. I know because it was not possible to love and care for Chris, nor he for me, until I had owned up to how bitter I was at being rejected by my own family. An awful realization to come to just months before the end, but it changed everything.

Pause.

Ted So what do I do?

Edwin You start asking questions.

Ted Like what?

Edwin Everything you want to know.

Ted Well, for . . .

Edwin It's not to say she's entirely blameless. . . .

Ted Damn right.

Edwin Nevertheless, sometimes you have to ask.

Ted In my books, that's prying.

Edwin Very Canadian.

Ted I figure, she wants to tell me stuff, she will.

Edwin Well, if you want her to make herself vulnerable to you, you have to be prepared to do the same yourself. Apostates, the pair of you.

Ted Apostates?

Edwin People who deny their calling, give up their faith.

Ted I didn't give up any faith.

Edwin You gave up physics, she gave up art. I want you to promise me something.

Ted Yeh?

Edwin Promise me you will give Suza's talent every possible opportunity you can muster.

Ted Yeh?

Edwin She must be allowed to develop, or I will haunt you till Doomsday.

Ted I guess. Sure. And this apostate business, does that include you?

Edwin No. . . . I'm a pilgrim.

Ted And what about the book, ol' buddy, ol' pal?

Edwin Pah! Scribblings of a half-wit. You can put them in the casket beside me.

SCENE TWO

Exterior / Interior—the dock and baitshop. Midafternoon.

A car is heard driving up. Mirek enters, pokes his head into the baitshop.

Mirek Ted? . . . Hallo, Ted?

He is carrying Jana's bag, which he puts on the dock. Jana enters. She has a new haircut, new clothes, looks different, vibrant, interesting. This is a reflection of her awakening artistic sense, not current fashion trends.

Jana Truck's gone. He must have gone to town. Looks like he was trying to hook up the plow.

Mirek Well . . . ?

Jana Sit. It's so warm.

Mirek You must have things to do.

Jana No.

Mirek You haven't seen your family for . . . ?

Jana What's the matter with you? No one is here. Sit for a while, enjoy the sun.

She sits. He stands uncertainly.

Pause.

Mirek How long is it to Toronto?

Jana Three, three and a half hours. Oh, it's so beautiful. Tomorrow could be winter again and forty below.

Mirek What are you going to do?

Jana God, I wish I knew. I feel like a giant encyclopedia with twenty years of unfiltered ideas and images jammed up inside of me. The problem is, I don't know if I speak the language anymore.

Mirek It's your mother tongue.

Jana Maybe I've lost it.

Mirek It'll come back.

Jana Will it?

Mirek Of course.

Jana Do I want it to?

He shrugs.

Pause.

Who am I? What do I look like?

An old lumberjack shirt of Ted's is on the bench. She puts it on, walks to the end of the dock and looks across the water.

Crystal Lake. I love this place, this lake, this life. Coming back here . . . I am safe, but . . . I am faceless.

Pause.

Tell me what to do, Mirku. I don't know what to do.

Mirek Don't panic. Don't create obstacles. Give yourself time. It'll come clear.

Jana Very good. This is the artist's manager speaking?

He shrugs.

Now I want to hear from Mirku, my friend.

Mirek You must find your own answers.

Jana Oh, come on, what's the matter with you today?

Mirek All right. You, Jana, must face your very great talent, a talent that comes with a responsibility in this. . . .

Jana Pah! Rhetoric! Rhetoric!

Mirek Nevertheless, the world is in a great state of . . .

Jana For God's sake, stop it! I want to know about you, what you feel.

Mirek Please, I don't want to influence you.

She bursts out laughing.

Jana You. You have been influencing me nonstop for a week . . . in some very interesting . . .

Mirek I don't mean that.

Jana No. And it's not funny.

Mirek No.

Jana Come on, talk to me, Mirku. Your life is here, too, is it not? May I not know what Mirek wants?

Mirek I don't think it's relevant.

Jana Only lies are irrelevant.

Pause.

Mirek I want you to come to New York with me. I want to be with you. I want to be there when you discover the excitement of being an artist again. I want to be there when you put your hands into the clay again and make it sing. I want see that reckless delight firing out of your eyes. I want to be there when your mind is so full of shapes and forms and images that you forget to eat and whistle tuneless nonsense through your teeth. I want to be the one to rub grease into your hands when they are dry and cracked. I want to see the world and every gallery in it with you and through your eyes. I want to sleep with you every night and make love with you again and again and again and again. I want you, Jana. I'm more in love with you now than I was twenty years ago. I want you.

Pause.

You asked.

Jana Yes.

Mirek I will be in Toronto for a few days and then Montreal. You can always reach me through Petr in Montreal.

Jana Mirku.

Mirek No, please.

He leaves. She watches him go.

Jana Damn you. I don't know. . . .

She turns to the lake.

Crystal Lake.

She walks down to the end of the dock.

A lifetime of questions, a hundred cries, sunk beneath your silent face.

She lies on the dock and reaches with her arms deep into the water.

Now I need answers, give me answers. . . .

Pause.

Ted appears silently at the top of the dock. She feels his presence and turns.

Ted.

Ted You're back

Pause.

They look each other.

New clothes.

She nods.

You look great.

Jana Thank you.

Ted We heard you on the radio.

Jana Oh, yes? did it sound okay?

Ted Yes, sure, quite a celebrity, eh?

Jana Sure. For a moment.

Ted So, what did you do in Ottawa?

Jana Lots and lots. A couple of concerts, a play. I spent three days in galleries. A couple of receptions, an interview in the paper . . . bought some books, tapes. Enough to feast on all winter long.

Pause.

Ted We missed you. Specially Bear. You glad to be back?

Jana Yes, of course.

Ted Where's Mirek?

Jana Gone, to Montreal . . . or Toronto.

Ted Already, huh?

Jana Yes, he rented a car, an appointment of some sort, I don't know.

Ted Well, that's good. I don't feel comfortable round him, you know.

Jana No kidding.

Ted He made me feel like a hick. I figure there's something not right about that.

Jana Oh, Ted, you play at being a hick.

Ted No, no, he made up his mind. He was real happy to dismiss me as being of no account.

Jana Ted. It doesn't suit you.

Ted What?

Jana Self-pity.

Ted I'm just telling you.

Jana You can't hold it against people when they take you up on the role you've chosen. It was you chose it.

Ted That's different. What I'm saying is he made a convenient snap . . .

Jana Ted! This is bullshit! You goaded him with being a hick. You goad me with it. Why do you do this? I don't understand.

Pause.

Ted I don't know you.

Jana What?

Ted You're different. I don't know you.

Jana Stop. My hair, new clothes . . .

Pause.

Ted That's it, then?

Jana What?

Ted He's gone to Montreal, you've come home. That's it?

Jana Mmmmmm.

Ted Everything's back to normal.

Jana I . . . I don't know.

Ted Oh? What does that mean?

Jana Please. It means I don't know.

Ted Didn't think it was gonna be that easy.

Jana A lot has happened. I'm confused.

Ted 'Bout what?

Jana I have some thinking to do.

Ted 'Bout what?

Jana About me, my life, art.

Ted I'm listening.

Jana Please, Ted . . . not now. I have to think.

Ted Fishing season's over.

Jana If you're trying to make me angry, you're succeeding. If you're trying to make me feel guilty, you're not.

Ted You sleep with him?

Pause.

Jesus!

Pause.

Jana I'm sorry.

Ted You're sorry?!

Jana I'm sorry to hurt you.

Ted Goddamn you!

Jana Please, Ted, try to be patient with me.

Ted Patient? Goddamn you! I been patient through God knows what all, till I've had it up to here. I been patient sixteen years, waiting for the day I can walk in that godamn door without worrying about what kind of goddamn mood you're gonna be in. And what do I get at the end of it? Some guy comes knocking on my door, some guy that happens to be your old lover, and takes you off and sacks you like some teenage hooker.

Jana You shit!

Ted You think I'm going to hang around here like some mongrel dog, waiting for you to decide who you like the best?

Jana Ted, please!

Ted This the way they do it back in Czechoslovakia, eh? Women are allowed to have lovers and make fools of their husbands, are they? They consider that reasonable, do they!?

Jana *Stop it!*

Pause.

Ted Okay, so maybe I haven't been fast enough asking the right questions all these years, but I think it's about time you started filling me in on a few things.

Pause.

Jana He's an old, old friend, Ted.

Ted Yeh, and I'm your husband.

Jana Look, it's not what you . . . you see, sleeping with him isn't . . . wasn't . . . *Oh, shit!* It's where we're coming from that you have to understand. We are connected, from a long time, he knows me through from my roots. He was able to wake me up, challenge me. He forced me to look at a part of me that has been silent for a long, long time. He knows how to touch an important part of . . .

Ted goes into the house. She follows.

Ted What a bunch of horseshit, Jan. You should hear yourself.

Jana You're not listening. You don't want to understand, do you?

Ted I don't want to listen to this bullshit!

Jana No, of course you don't. It might take you too close to confronting your own bullshit, to acknowledging you're no less half-dead than I am.

Ted What the hell are you talking about?

Jana You think you can cut off your right arm, just walk away and forget it, and expect everything to be all right? Wake up!

Ted I'm not the one goes fishing everytime someone says boo! I'm not the one out screwing old boy friends!

Jana Maybe you should be! Maybe you should be!

Pause.

He is still alive, all of him! He is still curious! He's not afraid to feel!

Ted And I am?

Jana Yes! You are, of my feelings, of your own feelings. He is not afraid of me, my blackness or my brilliance. I had forgotten that men and women can be emotional together, passionate, yell and scream and fight and laugh and cry and not be afraid, talk and talk and talk. I had forgotten what it was like to be awake in my mind and in my imagination. To feel again. I need this, I am starving for this. But . . . it is confusing as well. I don't know. . . . I don't know where it fits. . . . I don't know what it means . . . for you and me, don't you see? . . . What it means, what to do . . .

Don't force me, Ted, don't force me to come to . . .

Ted Don't insult me, Jan, by trying to pin it on me. If that's what you want, you're starving for, then you better go do it. I can't compete, not with that.

Jana Do you want to? Do you? What do you want out of this marriage, Ted? Do you know what you want, feel even, from one minute to the next?

Ted I'm just tired, real tired of trying to figure things out all the time, what you want. I don't know for sure but it sounds like you want someone different, not me.

Jana Things never change, do they? I don't think you ever really hear what I'm saying, do you?

Ted Okay, I'm askin'. What the hell are you trying to say to me? I'm listening, okay? I'm here. Make me understand.

Jana I keep reaching for you. I keep trying to pull you. But you won't move. Or no . . . it's like I'm climbing up these stairs to a hallway full of doors, and just as I'm getting to the top, you slam all the doors shut. I have to go through one of them. I've been standing on this landing too long. I'm stuck. I'm stale. I'm afraid. I don't want to go, but you've locked all the doors. I want to go on.

Ted Why is it always my fault? Why am I always wrong?

A doors slams open. Suza enters.

Jana But don't you see, it's both of us. I'm wrong, too. Don't you understand? I'm wrong, too. We're stuck, both of us.

Ted Just decide what you're gonna do.

Suza 'Bout what? Whoa, look what the cat dragged in. When'd you get back?

Jana Just a little while.

Pause.

Ted Where's Bear?

Suza He got off at Jergen's place. Says he doesn't like coming home to an empty house.

Ted Oh, he did, did he?

Suza What's wrong?

Ted Well, he'd better get used to it. Now I'm gonna have to go get him.

He exits.

Suza Mum?

Jana I have to get changed.

Suza Mum! What's going on?

Jana Your father and I had a fight.

Suza No kidding. What about?

Jana It's not your business.

Suza I think it is. Mum! Talk to me!

Jana stops and looks at her.

Jana All right. I might be going, for a while, to Montreal . . . or New York . . . for a while.

Suza I get it. That where Mirek is?

Jana Yes.

Suza You can't do that.

Jana Oh?

Suza This is our family, you can't just walk out. We need you.

Jana And what about what I need?

Suza Like what?

Jana I need a life that is mine. I need to work again as an artist.

Suza You can be an artist right here.

Jana You know nothing about it.

Suza So explain.

Jana Not now, Suza, please.

Suza *Yes, now! Talk to me!*

Jana Suza . . .

Suza If you're walking out on us, I have a right to understand why.

Jana You have no right to . . .

Suza You've been fucking him, haven't you? This isn't about art, this is about fucking!

Jana Suza!

Suza What about us? What about Daddy? You get bored with Daddy, is that it? Don't we mean anything?

Jana Of course you do, Suza. You mean the whole world . . .

Suza No we don't, you're not here for us. You're never here.

Jana That's not true and you know it. You two and Daddy are the only things in my life. I'm always here—always, always. I never go away.

Suza Oh, yeh, sure, in body, but in spirit? In your mind? You're somewhere else. Okay, so I'm not the perfect daughter, I'm stubborn and arrogant and all that, but I need you, you're my Mother and you have no right to abandon me . . . no right. I need you.

Jana Suza, what's wrong, what is this?

Suza breaks down.

Suza Shit. Shit. Shit.

Jana Suza, Suza, something's happened. What is this?

Suza It's so stupid, so stupid. They did it, Mama, they actually did it. They picked Gerald Humbolt for the National Debate. I'm not going. Gerald Humbolt! Can you believe that? He's a no-brain, Mum, a total no-brain! He thinks perastroika is a kind of polish sausage, for God's sake. He'll humiliate us.

Jana Oh, Suza.

Suza Don't they understand what I was trying to tell them? I was living it, Mum. Democracy, democratic freedom . . . I was living freedom of choice, freedom of expression.

Jana I know, my Suza, I know, but all they saw was a stubborn, teenager. Oh, Suza, I'm so sorry, so sor—

Suza No, you're not. You're smug and pleased. You're thinking, "I told you so." Go ahead, say, "I told you so."

Jana I told you so.

Suza How can you say that to me?

Jana But it's true, Suza, I did and you wouldn't listen.

Suza How can I listen to you, you're so, you're so . . . emotional, so dramatic, so East European.

Jana Yes, you're right, it's me. I should be different.

Suza I slaughtered Gerald Humbolt in the debate. I mean, I totally slaughtered him. Why would they choose to send someone who isn't even smart? It's so back-assed.

Jana Because they have to prove that they won't be pushed around by a young girl.

Suza Why does that even have to matter? The point I was making, and any bimbo can see it . . . the point I was . . .

Jana Yes, I know, what you were trying to say and do was right, theoretically. But you didn't handle them right. You have to learn to be . . .

Suza No. I won't do that. You're the one that's always on about being honest and truthful.

Jana If you want to go out on a limb with truth and justice, go ahead. But be realistic about the consequences.

Suza Why should I pussyfoot around being diplomatic and manipulative when the political truth is staring them in the face?

Jana This world is not a just place. Accept it. Accept the consequences of your actions. Learn it now.

Suza It's like agreeing to live with lies. I hate it!

Jana Not everybody has the same passion and imagination you have. It's wonderful to be passionate and imaginative, but be wise, too, and realistic.

Suza It's disgusting! I hate it! I bet my grandfather never compromised.

Jana And he suffered for it, you cannot imagine, and so did we.

Pause.

When I was, oh, younger than you, ten or twelve, we used to go, Dela and Mama and I on the train, long journeys to see him in jail. A tired, grey man in a tired grey room. We had to kiss him. The tears would run down over his chin under his collar, but he never made a sound. Then we would go on the train again, all the way home. Mama would sing and cry quietly to herself, and we would sleep in her lap. I used to wonder if he had known the terrible consequences of standing so rigidly by his beliefs, if he would have done it again.

Suza And would he, do you think?

Jana Yes, probably. I think so. He was passionately idealistic. You come by those qualities honestly, my Suza.

Pause.

Suza Mum, you look fab, you really do.

Jana Thank you.

Suza Are you going to leave?

Jana I don't know.

Suza Did you really go to bed with . . . you know, Mirek?

Jana Yes, I did.

Suza So you don't love Daddy anymore?

Jana No, that's not what it means. My love for him did not change one bit.

Suza Then why? I don't understand.

Jana No.

Suza Mum?

Jana I can't explain. How can I explain . . . I . . . ? Maybe when your father has calmed down he can.

Suza Yeh?

Jana It hurts him a lot, but I think he understands. In any event, some day you will understand on your own.

Pause.

You'll never guess who I heard playing in Ottawa.

Suza Who?

Jana Josef Suk.

Suza Mum! Oh, Mum! . . . Was he wonderful?

Jana Yes, he was. I wished so much you were there.

Suza What did he play?

Jana The Sibelius Concerto.

Suza Oh, Mum!

Jana I bought you the tape, but it's with the Berlin Philharmonic, not the NAC Orchestra. It's probably better.

She takes it out her pocker and gives it to her. Bear and Ted come in the back door. Bear rushes to Jana and throws his arms around her.

Bear I love you, Mum. I love you very, very much.

Jana looks at Ted.

Ted I haven't told him a thing.

Bear I know you're probably going to have to go away, Mum, but I don't want you to.

Jana looks at Ted again.

Ted I swear, I haven't said a thing.

Jana Hush, little bear. The sky is not falling.

Bear Tell me you won't go. Promise.

Jana Oh, Bear, I don't think you would want me to make easy promises.

Ted Suza!

Suza What?

Ted stomps out.

Ted Come help fix dinner.

Jana Why are you so sure I'm leaving, Bear?

Bear I knew when I heard you on the radio. All of a sudden it just made sense.

Jana What?

Bear Well, you.

Ted Suza!

Suza Just wait, Dad!

Jana I don't understand.

Bear It's like you keep dumping sand on top. It's like . . . well . . . it's like there's something wet and messy and . . . and you keep sort of burying it . . . like dumping sand on top . . . but no matter how much you put on, the wet keeps coming back up. Then when Mirek came, it just all sort of broke open and exploded. I know it probably doesn't make any sense.

Jana It makes a lot of sense, Bear, a lot of sense.

Bear So, are you going to go away?

Jana I don't know, I don't know. I don't know if I can leave you, you and Suza and Daddy, I don't know if I can. I need a little time to think, I guess.

Bear But you might have to.

Jana Yes, I might.

He puts his arms around her.

Suza Don't leave, Mum, don't leave.

Jana Oh, Suza.

Suza He's just an old boy friend.

Jana Yes, and he's rather sad, isn't he. He carries me like a beacon before him.

Pause.

Bear Ma, when they raided the barn?

Jana Yes?

Ted comes to the doorway and stays to the end of the scene.

Bear You saw them? You were there?

Jana Yes.

Bear What . . . what was it like? Did they see you?

Jana No.

Pause.

I was sweeping. I remember the sun slanting across from

the window; the dust particles lifting into the shaft of light, the table with snow white cloth and sparkling champagne glasses . . . it was a beautiful . . . the barn, old, and the pictures and tapestries and sculptures placed . . . so . . . and so. I heard a van drive up. I looked out the window and I . . . I . . . my stomach . . . I knew what was . . . I climbed up into the loft and hid.

Bear What did they do?

Jana They were drunk. They tore every painting, photograph and tapestry off the wall and with fists and axes destroyed them. They smashed every piece of sculpture, broke every window, every piece of furniture. They laughed and shouted and cursed. One of them, the youngest, so young he didn't have a beard, he was vomiting all the time. They pulled the door off it's hinges, and then they . . . they pissed on everything . . . and with my eyes and ears I witnessed every single moment of it.

Bear And your sculptures were . . .

Jana Like the rest. It was like watching my children being slaughtered.

Pause.

Bear Boy! It sure is a good thing the communists have all gone.

Jana There are many different ways for governments to silence artists.

Bear *But why?

Suza *Why?

Jana Because they tell the truth. Artists are truth tellers.

Suza God!

Pause.

Bear Ma, if you promise you'll come back, it's okay . . . if you have to go away for a while . . . it's okay.

Jana Oh, Bear . . . my little grizzly bear.

They hold onto each other.

Pause.

Fade to black.

SCENE THREE

Exterior, dock area. Night.

Suza can be heard doing violin excercies in the house—scales, etc.

Jana is seen as a dark figure huddled on the bench by the baitshop door. The door opens. Ted comes out. He remains apart from her.

Ted Seems to me we gotta separate which are your problems and which you figure are my problems.

See, I don't think you should leave. I mean, it just wouldn't be right, for the kids and all. Maybe when the kids are on their own more. But not now, it wouldn't be right. Okay? There's stuff we gotta figure out, I know, but . . .

How can you say I don't have any feelings? How can you say that? How can that be true?

No answer.

I was angry, real angry when I found out you . . . when I found out. I know it's not the same, but who wouldn't be? Eh? That's just being normal and healthy.

But now I want to talk, really talk. I want to listen. I've never been one to pry and ask questions, that's just my way and I can see now that it's not a good way . . . and . . . I guess I just kinda forgot about how much I don't know about you, your past. I mean, I can't believe none of us knew anything about that business in the barn. Gees, Jan. Did Otto know at least? Jan?

Jana I don't know.

Ted How can you just not tell me something that important about yourself? Maybe if I'd known, I'd have been able to be more . . . more . . . I don't know, more what? What do you need me to be more of? I spend my whole goddamn life trying to figure out what you need! I can't do it anymore, Jan. It doesn't help.

Maybe you should go. Or . . . what if we all went, yeh, just close up shop and move to the city. I could get a teaching job, Suza'd get a new music teacher, you could . . . you could . . . No, that's not the point, is it? Or is it? Maybe if . . .?

Help me, Jan.

I do have feelings. I know I have feelings. I must have feelings.

Goddamn it to hell! Don't I get a few goddamned points for trying, at least? I have tried so bloody hard to make you happy, to be a good husband, father, to make a good life for us. I don't know what else to do! I've tried everything I know how, I really have, I've done my best. And here we are, come to this . . . this . . . and you're telling me I don't have any feelings! I don't even know what you mean. It's just not true, I've got feelings, for God's sake, I have feelings, like right now I've got . . . I'm . . . I . . . You wanna know what I'm feeling right now? . . . I'm . . . I've . . . I've got a fucking stomachache, that's what.

No. I know what it is. I feel betrayed. I feel like all these years, you've had a secret lover I knew nothing about, not just Mirek, everything, the whole thing. There's a whole other you I know nothing about, and it pisses me off. Okay, so I didn't ask, it's my fault for not digging, but I thought that was the right way to be. A person is entitled to privacy in their minds at least. I knew there was someone, someone before me. You even told me about him, but I thought it was over before you came here. Is that what this is about, Jan? That it's not over, that you're still in love with him? Am I just beating myself black and blue for no reason? That's not it, is it?

I need to know, Jan.

No. No. I won't go for that. You can't tell me this is a lousy marriage and I didn't notice. I'm not such a lout. I don't accept that. We can work this out, I know we can. I can't just let you go, just like that. I don't want to live that way . . . without you . . . I love you . . . and I'm scared . . . I'm scared . . . you're going to leave me.

He breaks down.

Don't leave me. Please don't leave, Jan. I need you. You keep me human. You keep me real. I'll turn into a cardboard person if you go, and how can I bring up the kids and love them if I'm made of cardboard, a cutout? I know, I know I've failed you when you get down and depressed and can't cope. I know I'm not there for you, I'm no good I back off, I know, because . . . because I know. I know where you are, I do know, Jan, down underneath all those layers of cardboard, I know all about it, and it scares the shit out of me, scares the shit right out of me because if I breathe too deep, I'll . . . I'll . . . I'll be there, too . . . and then where will we be? Huh? I just can't let myself do that, can't let myself go. Someone's gotta keep us standing upright.

Jana comes down and sits by him, not facing but in physical contact with him. We hear Suza working on the opening phrases of the Sibelius concerto. They listen.

Pause.

Ted That the tape you gave her? The Sibelius?

Jana Mmmmmm.

Pause.

Ted You're right what you said. I did, I cut off my own right arm when I left all those . . . those scientific riddles behind. I tried to run away from a part of what makes me tick, and little by little I'm turning into cardboard. Maybe what it is, is . . . here comes a second chance at your life, a second chance to do what you set out to do in the first place, and it drives me crazy.

Pause.

They listen to Suza working on the phrase.

She's gettin' it. She's real good, isn't she. She's special.

Jana Mmmmmm.

Ted I keep thinking of that dream you had. You know, the onion?

Pause.

Oh, Jan, it's you keeps me warm, keeps me alive.

Edwin is heard approaching, singing drunkenly.

Edwin The bells of Hell go
Ting a ling a ling
For you but not for me.
Oh, death where is thy
Sting a ling a ling
Or grave thy victory.

Violin louder as she tries the phrase again. Edwin listens.

The keening of angels . . . Ah, Suza . . . my brilliant Suza. Shut the bloody row up there! How the hell's a fellow s'posed to keep his bloody equilibrium?

He lets out a roar.

"Do not go gentle into that good night.
Rage, rage against the . . . "

He overbalances.

Whoops. Bloody hell. . . .

He raises an imaginary glass in a toast.

Thank you, Comrads. Friends at the tap. Companions, in an hour of utterly shallow, base and tasteless passing of a cool autumn evening. Ah, where would I be without thee, salt of the earth. . . . Fillers of the outhouse. . . . Defilers of the earth . . . who snigger like snotty schoolboys at my retreating rear. Egits, I know the fool you think me. Philistines! Rye and Coke drinkers! Look how plodding and crass your world is, no mystery, no light. No, no, I'm never the fool, no, no, no. I am . . . only the clown . . .

He is sober, suddenly.

. . . in my longing . . . in my wistfulness, and barren as an old spinster. Though they be made invisible and mute in a numb and careless world, I would be one of them—the poets, the dreamspeakers, the lost voice of angels, whose questions glimpse heaven.

Suza gets the phrase right, moves onto the next.
He listens.

"Synopsis of the Soul . . . "

Pause.

Jana stands.

Jana In the translucent centre of the onion layers, a mirror, like a gift, a jewel, a tiny, silver mirror. Yes, I think, yes, I'm going to find my little Soviet peasant doll, the one I lost so long ago. How wonderful. I look into the mirror and . . . there is nothing, it is empty, there is nothing there. I have no face? Where are my eyes, my nose, my mouth? Who am I? Where have I gone? I put my hands up to my face to find . . . hard, cold lumps of dead clay. I begin to weep, hot tears running, running, running down the cold clay, making it wet, all wet and my hands, of ancient habit begin to warm the clay, to knead it, shape it, to thrill and sing, and when I look again in the tiny mirror I see a face begin to form—rough, angular, primeval features, the underside of a rock. And in my hands, the clay is warming now, pliable, willing, and I know that I can make again my face.

Slow fade as Suza is heard playing Sibelius.

fin.